# IMPERIAL LETTERS TO THE SPANISH & VENETIANS

# IMPERIAL LETTERS TO THE SPANISH & VENETIANS

ANDRONICUS II PALAIOLOGOS

Copyright 2025 by Dalcassian Press

All rights reserved. No part of this book may be reproduced in any manner whatsoever without written permission except in the case of brief quotations embodied in critical articles and reviews.

No part of this publication may be reproduced, distributed, or transmitted in any form or by any means, including photocopying, recording, or other electronic or mechanical methods, without the prior written permission of the publisher, except in the case of brief quotations embodied in critical reviews and certain other non-commercial uses permitted by copyright law. For permission request, write to Dalcassian Press at admin@thescriptoriumproject.com

Translator: Curtin, D.P. (1985-)
Translator: Papadopolos, J (1947-)

ISBN: 979-8-3493-8708-1 (Paperback)
ISBN: 979-8-3493-4673-6 (eBook)
Library of Congress Control Number:

Printed by Ingram Content Group, 1 Ingram Blvd, La Vergne, Tennessee
First Printing 2025, Dalcassian Press, Wilmington, DE

This work is part of a series produced in association with the Scriptorium Project and its community of scholars and translators.
Please visit our website at: www.thescriptoriumproject.com

# 1

# LETTER ONE

**Unknown, 1290 AD**
*Emperor Andronicus Palaeologus grants privileges to the Spanish merchants.*

Since the inhabitants of the region of Parezalona, of Ragusa, of Catalonia, of Mallorca, of Valencia, of Tortosa, and of other territories of the most high lord of Ragusa and Sicily have made a petition to my kingdom through the arrival here in Constantinople of the consul of the Catalans, the wise man Sir Dalmain Suner, as some of them desire to settle both in Constantinople and in other lands of theirs and to conduct business therein, they have requested and implored that they be granted a golden bull from my majesty, in order to have permission for this and to come without hindrance, and for them to also have some governance regarding the return of commerce. My kingdom, having considered their request and appeal, grants this present golden bull to them, through which it is also established that the mentioned settlers of the region of Parezalona, of Ragusa, of Catalonia, of Mallorca, of Valencia, of Tortosa, and of other nearby lands of the most high lord of Ragusa and Sicily may dwell in Constantinople and in other lands of my kingdom, whenever they wish, and all who among them choose this, and to conduct therein the businesses they deem fit without disturbance and without oppression, to pay the due fees for commerce for the importation of three hundred hyperpyra, and for exportation also three other hyperpyra, and not to be subjected to any more, but rather to be maintained safe both in their persons and in their affairs, and to suffer no other harm or oppression or plunder from any of all those from my kingdom. Furthermore, as they have also requested regarding this, if it happens that their ship encounters danger at sea from a storm and comes ashore in the territory of my kingdom, the inhabitants of such a land or any others shall not come to seize and take anything from their salvaged goods, but rather to safeguard such a thing will be preserved unchanged, by the power and strength of the present golden bull of my kingdom. For by its appearance, they will be maintained unharmed and without loss after the giving of the written document, and they will not suffer any injustice or damage or any kind of harm and attack from anyone. For this reason, the present golden bull of my kingdom has come into being, and it has been rewarded and granted to the mentioned settlers of Parzalonas, of Ragounas, of Catalonia, of Mallorca, of Valencia, of Tortosa, and of the other surrounding regions of the most high lord Ragounas and Sicily for confirmation and security.

# 2

# LETTER TWO

**Unknown, 1320 AD**

*Emperor Andronicus Palaeologus grants privileges to the Spanish merchants.*

Since the most exalted lord Ragounas, of Valencia, Sardinia, Corsica, the noble Bartzelona, and the most cherished divine of my kingdom, Jacob the choir, sent to my kingdom his letter with the Catalan merchants, namely Beregarius, Bonatus Renzis, Guglielmo Bertolini, and Tomasi and Podio, indicating to my kingdom that, for the love towards him and the genuine affection of my kingdom, these merchants should receive from my kingdom a guarantee of unhindered activity in their dealings in his land, and furthermore my kingdom ordains that both they and the others from their land who will come to the territories of my kingdom for dealings should also enjoy the same unhindered activity. My kingdom not only readily and willingly accepted this, but along with this, for the love and genuine affection that it has towards the same most exalted lord and cherished divine of my kingdom, it has distinguished and ordained to have greater governance. They are to be given in return for the owed payment from them for their trade, as they had before, and they are already making a cut from that trade from which they had the usual practice and were giving, as has been said, previously. For the present golden bull of hers releases them, by which it is ordained to reside without hindrance the aforementioned traders and others, as many as wish to come here from the mentioned country of the most high lord and divine protector of my kingdom, to both the Theotokos, the great and God-protected Constantinople, and to the other lands of my kingdom, whenever they wish, and to conduct their trade there without interruption and without oppression, to repay debts owed for trade above the hundred overpasses, and for the export likewise two other overpasses, and not to be drawn into a greater payment, but rather to be maintained more safely both to their bodies and their affairs and to suffer no other loss, oppression, or plunder from anyone of all those from the part of my kingdom. As for the requests made by such traders regarding this matter, if it should happen that their ship encounters danger at sea from a storm and runs aground in the land of my kingdom, the colonists of such a country or any others shall not come to seize and profit from what remains of their affairs, but such a matter shall be preserved unaltered, since whoever dares to cause harm to them, the shipwrecked traders, and to take something from their goods, shall be obliged to repay and satisfy and restore in full whatever is taken, and to be punished as the present golden bull of my kingdom dictates; for by this manifest decree shall all traders from the mentioned country of Catalonia be maintained undisturbed after the granting of the written trade license and shall not suffer any injustice or damage or harassment and assault of any kind. For this reason, this present golden bull of my kingdom has been granted and awarded to the mentioned traders and others, as many as are from the mentioned country of the declared divine protector of my kingdom, the most high Rhegus, they will wish to begin here and in the other lands of my kingdom, for confirmation and defense and safety.

# LETTER THREE

**In the month of October 1324, indiction VIII. In Venice.**

*Emperor Andronicus senior extends the previous agreements made for five years, promising compensation for the damages inflicted on them by the Greeks.*

[In the name of the Lord, Amen. Since] my kingdom has sent the most reverend esteemed servant to it, lord [Stephen the Suroplon to the illustrious duke and the commune of Venice as an envoy and ambassador, having the power through the aforementioned procuratorial golden bull to negotiate, agree, restore, and fulfill; new treaties between our kingdom and the same illustrious duke and the commune of Venice, and from there he arrived and agreed with them and restored and fulfilled treaties of all years, commencing from the eleventh of the past June of the seventh indiction, so that it may confirm all the agreements and the provisions, which have been made in the preceding treaties between my kingdom and the illustrious duke and the commune of Venice, to be rectified and some of them, concerning which it will be stated more clearly, which will also be indicated below, the aforementioned our ambassador promised and swore that my kingdom would confirm and uphold this written sworn agreement, which it agreed upon and established and restored, my kingdom, confirming as far as the aforementioned ambassador agreed and swore, having the license and power to do so through the aforementioned procuratorial golden bull, the present sworn agreement of it is already set forth, [since he swears by the holy Gospels of God] and by the venerable and life-giving cross, and he affirms, [that he may confirm unchangeably and immovably all that he established and agreed upon and restored, the aforementioned] our ambassador along with the stated illustrious duke and the commune of Venice regarding the stipulated duration of five years, namely, to keep a pure and unblemished treaty for us and our kingdom towards the illustrious duke and [the commune of Venice and towards all their part, and let us guard all the aforementioned chapters, which are included in the previously mentioned treaties. [Likewise, also the now] corrected from the aforementioned chapters, that is, so that all the Venetians and those who are considered Venetians and those associated with them may have freedom in [all the territory of our] kingdom to buy and trade the produce from the greater [sea and all other grain, that which is not cultivated, namely in the lands of the kingdom [of ours and to sell such] grain, wherever they wish and it seems good to them in [the lands of my kingdom], freely and without the burden of [the place of the offering of the most glorious God, the great God, the God-protected] Constantinople, freely and without any burden [or hindrance, but the grain that is cultivated in the] land of my kingdom is found in the [land, as is included in the previous treaties. Furthermore, so that all the Venetians and those [who are considered Venetians and are] accounted as Venetians may have the license and freedom to export, [transport, buy and sell] in all the regions of the land of our kingdom, millet, beans, [barley and all other] produce and pulses, without the grain that is cultivated in the [land of my kingdom, as] is included in the previous treaties, and so that they may [freely and unobstructedly export all the aforementioned goods by both the Venetians [and those who are considered Venetians, without] the usual [imposition of customs, taxes, burdens or any other possible hindrance or obstruction that could arise or be conceived. Furthermore, so that my kingdom is obliged to compensate for any [damage occurring] to the Venetians [and those associated] with them and those accounted as Venetians due to military actions [or military actions occurring or arising in the regions of my kingdom, from which even if they may occur to Romans, [Latins, or any other] lineage. That concerning the damages suffered by the Venetians and those subject to the illustrious duke and the commune of Venice from the people [and those subject to my kingdom, so that my kingdom may give a total of twelve thousand hyperpyra in gold within the period of three years, after the harvest, from the eleventh of the aforementioned month of June, [from which the pre-mentioned event began], it started, namely, each year for four thousand hyperpyra, [until the twelve thousand hyperpyra are fully paid], for which reason both the illustrious donor and the communal authority of Venice relinquish and nullify all damage and harm incurred by all those of the part [of the people and the part] of my kingdom until the eleventh of the aforementioned month of June, [and liberate forever the aforementioned damages of] my kingdom and its people; likewise, [my kingdom relinquishes and nullifies] any harm and damage that has occurred by the aforementioned [illustrious donor and the communal authority of Venice or by these captains or some other officials and others subjected to them against the Romans and subjected to my kingdom, and to] liberate forever the illustrious duke and all those subject to him, [being preserved and saved from the rights and claims and debts of the declared Venetians, namely the debt] of the noble man Peter Mauros from Saint Augustine, demanding three thousand hyperpyra, given through him as a loan to the son-in-law of our kingdom, to that Palaiologos at that table when he was found in Ioannina. Also [the demand and debt of Paul Kontarinos, acting on behalf of the noble men Balianos and Marino Kontarinos. Also of Stephen Badouaros, being active on behalf of the nobleman Jacob of Bandeligos for the sake of hyperpyra of two thousand four hundred and ten at twelve hyperpyra for each, given also as a loan to the aforementioned at the table, to Palaiologos, from which amount he must be retained, as much as he received from the transactions of those whom he held as collateral, regarding which examination must be believed the letters of the batoulou and his advisors, who made such collateral sold by order of the illustrious duke of Venice. As for the demand of the noble man Thomas de Menzo, demanding without penalties and expenses four thousand hyperpyra and two hundred and seven hyperpyra for twenty hands of Turinese for each hyperpyron through certain compromises and agreements that he had with the most revered household of my kingdom, Criton, who is according to the Peloponnese of Theophorites, of the lord Michael the cavalier of Sofia, still regarding the demand and debt of Nikolaos Fouskoulo and Simeon Kourmoulidis, demanding three thousand hyperpyra and nine hundred nineteen hyperpyra and four strilings for twenty hands of turners, for each hyperpyron by agreement, which he had with the mentioned relative of the kingdom of mine, the dance of Andronikos Palaiologos. That regarding the demand and debt of the aforementioned Simeon Kourmoulidis, demanding two hundred eighty liters and fourteen soldia, also one hundred hyperpyra for twenty hands of turners by agreement, which he had with the mentioned relative of the kingdom of mine, for which my kingdom owes five demands and debts according to the previous promise of the aforementioned ambassador of my kingdom, the most venerable and respected relative, lord Stephanos Syropoulos, to be arranged to become full and exact justice within the passage of one year, starting from the beginning of last September of the eighth indiction, according to the summary of the letters and proofs, which they received and have from the aforementioned lords and heads and offenders of my kingdom. If within the declared time the aforementioned lenders do not arrive for the proper justice and satisfaction according to the summary of their documents, after the time has passed, my kingdom is immediately liable to provide satisfaction to them from its treasury up to the group of the included capital in their documents. Also regarding the stated term of five years of the recently made treva, in order for so much additional time to proceed, as it is clear that both parties agree, namely my kingdom and the distinguished duke and the commune of Venice; but if my kingdom or the distinguished duke himself and the commune of Venice, after the declared period of five years, wishes to dissolve such a treva, so that it may have in any part the freedom to dissolve it, but not otherwise, unless first the mentioned part is dissolved, it shall declare and make known and manifest that nothing is preferred to be further involved in this treva. Then, after such declaration and manifestation, it must be presented for another six-month period, and for a time to the [travan, so that] those who are from the part of my kingdom may return to the parts [of the illustrious duke] and the commune of Venice, and those who are from the part of the [such Venetians] may return to the parts of my kingdom, each to his own, and may remain unharmed and unscathed during such a duration [of six months. All these] things, as are contained in the present oath, my kingdom shall uphold and protect, just as the illustrious duke of Venice is also to make a written document similar to this oath and to swear it upon his soul and the souls of all from the part and the commune of [Venice] according to his custom before those who are to come or the sending away that is to happen from my kingdom regarding this matter, and to send it with him to my kingdom, as he has promised and pledged, and to uphold and confirm all and each of the said matters. Therefore, for the sake of all these things, this present oath has been established and has come to be a golden bull of my kingdom, and my kingdom has sworn this in the presence of her nephew, lord Andronikos Palaiologos of the Asanites, and of the nephew of my kingdom, lord Konstantinos Palaiologos of the Asanites, and of the nephew of my kingdom, the great logothete lord Theodoros Metochites, and of the nephew of my kingdom, the protovestiarios lord Andronikos Kantakouzene, and of the nephew of my kingdom, the great papios lord Konstantinos Palaiologos, and of the nephew of my kingdom, the great drungarios of the vigil lord Dimitrios Palaiologos of Tornike, and this was given to the noble man, the lord Thomas Souvrantzis, by the hands of my kingdom according to the request of the illustrious duke of Venice, written in Roman letters by the hand of the notary of my kingdom, Michael Klostomallos, and in Latin by the one from the interpreters of my kingdom, Georgios Kavallaropoulos, in the month of October of the present eighth indiction of the sixteenth thousand eight hundred thirty-third year according to our enumeration, and according to the custom of the Latins from the incarnation of our Lord Jesus Christ in the year of the 1324, it was usually confirmed by the red personal signature of my kingdom and secured by a golden seal placed below.

Andronicus, faithful king and emperor of the Romans, Palaiologos.

This work was produced in association with:

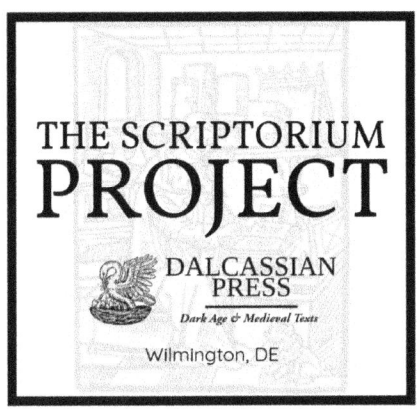

www.ingramcontent.com/pod-product-compliance
Lightning Source LLC
LaVergne TN
LVHW061050070526
838201LV00074B/5247